LIFE'S LITTLE
REMINDERS

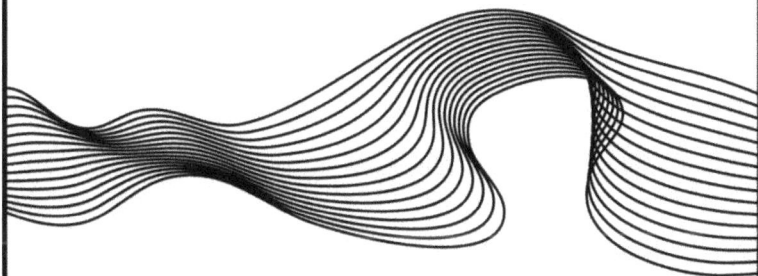

Victoria M. Goodman

LIFE'S LITTLE REMINDERS

CYOR Publications

ISBN: 0991511824
ISBN-13: 978-0-9915118-2-2

www.vyktohria.com

For Jennifer who always believed in me, who inspires me constantly, and who taught me to believe in the magical again. Always more sparkles—never not more sparkles!

For Bryan, one of the kindest and most loving souls I've ever met. It's taken me a half a lifetime to find you, let's spend the second half holding hands and counting stars.

PREFACE

Social media has become an indispensable part of modern life. It allows us to stay in touch with friends and family all over the world, while being a place where new friendships can be made and information about world events transmitted instantaneously. At the same time, studies are beginning to emerge about the potentially harmful emotional and psychological effects social media sites may have on individuals. When I noticed my own emotional well-being becoming negatively affected by online social websites, I decided to filter my social media so that only those people and things that made me laugh and feel good on a regular basis showed up on my feeds. It wasn't long before the constant stream of positive sayings and images took effect. I noticed a marked change for the better in my general frame of mind, and I knew this feeling was something I wanted others to feel as well. I have taken some of the best quotes, sayings and true-isms of life that I came across and compiled them here in this book to share with you. I hope they bring you as much joy and self-assurance as they continue to bring me.

- *Victoria*

Let go,
and
Let in.

Seek to be worth
knowing rather than
be well known.

Die with
memories
not
dreams.

SOMETIMES YOU DON'T REALIZE
YOU'RE ACTUALLY DROWNING
WHEN YOU'RE TRYING TO BE
EVERYONE ELSE'S ANCHOR.

You matter.

LEARN TO SAY
"NO" WITHOUT
EXPLAINING
YOURSELF.

NEVER GIVE
SOMEONE THE
OPPORTUNITY TO
WASTE YOUR
TIME TWICE.

ARE YOU REALLY LIVING LIFE, OR ARE YOU JUST
PAYING BILLS UNTIL YOU DIE?

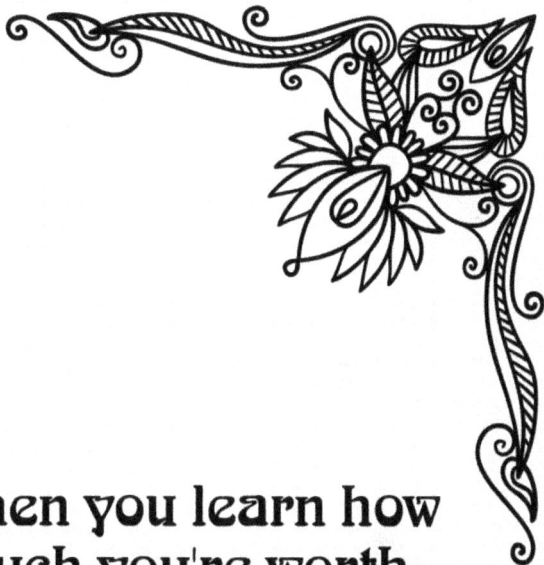

When you learn how much you're worth, you'll stop giving people discounts.

THE FIRST STEP TO
GETTING WHAT YOU
WANT IS HAVING THE
COURAGE TO GET RID OF
WHAT YOU DON'T.

DON'T BELIEVE
THOSE WHO
TELL YOU THEY
LOVE YOU.
BELIEVE THOSE
WHO SHOW
YOU THEY DO.

WALKING AWAY
FROM SOMETHING
THAT BRINGS YOU
DOWN IS
COURAGEOUS, EVEN
IF YOUR KNEES ARE
SHAKING.

10 WAYS TO REDUCE NEGATIVITY IN YOUR LIFE:

1. Don't take other people's negativity seriously.

2. Spend more time with positive people.

3. Be the positivity you want to see in the world.

4. Change the way you think.

5. Focus on solutions.

6. Love whomever is around to be loved.

7. Show you care.

8. Accept that life has its ups and downs.

9. Be in the present.

10. Let go and move on.

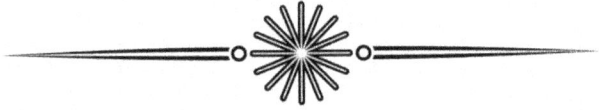

Do not, I repeat, **do not** allow anyone
to sit high and look low to judge you.
Everyone has a chapter in their life
they don't read out loud.

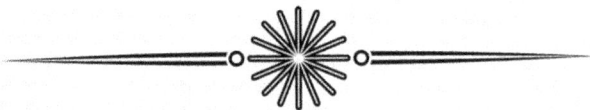

Goals are
dreams with
deadlines.

Don't be afraid of being different. Be afraid of being the same as everyone else.

Closure is a joke. The only apology you need is the one you owe yourself for staying as long as you did. The only conversation you need to have and the only person you need to see again is the person in the mirror. Look at yourself and say, "You know what? I fucked up. My worth is more than that." That's your closure. Don't keep dancing with the devil and wonder why you are still in hell.

Be careful
who you
pretend to be.
You might
forget who you
are.

YOU WILL
NEVER HAVE
TO FORCE
ANYTHING
THAT'S TRULY
MEANT TO BE.

KEEP ASKING
YOURSELF:

WHAT CAN I
LEARN FROM
THIS
SITUATION?

Loving somone who doesn't love you back is like hugging a cactus. The tighter you hold on, the more it hurts.

In case nobody told
you today, you are
good enough.

12 STEPS TO SELF CARE:

1. IF IT FEELS WRONG, DON'T DO IT.

2. SAY EXACTLY WHAT YOU MEAN.

3. DON'T BE A PEOPLE PLEASER.

4. TRUST YOUR INSTINCTS.

5. NEVER SPEAK BAD ABOUT YOURSELF.

6. NEVER GIVE UP YOUR DREAMS.

7. DON'T BE AFRAID TO SAY "NO."

8. DON'T BE AFRAID TO SAY "YES."

9. BE KIND TO YOURSELF.

10. LET GO OF WHAT YOU CAN'T CONTROL.

11. STAY AWAY FROM DRAMA AND NEGATIVITY.

12. LOVE.

Fools take a knife and stab people in the back. The wise take a knife, cut the cord and set themselves free from the fools.

The biggest regret
that people have on
their deathbed is that
they lived the life
expected of them
instead of a life true
to themselves.

Monsters don't sleep under your bed. They sleep inside your head.

DO EPIC SHIT.

The greatest achievement in life is to have the ability to create the world around you so that it matches the dreams in your mind.

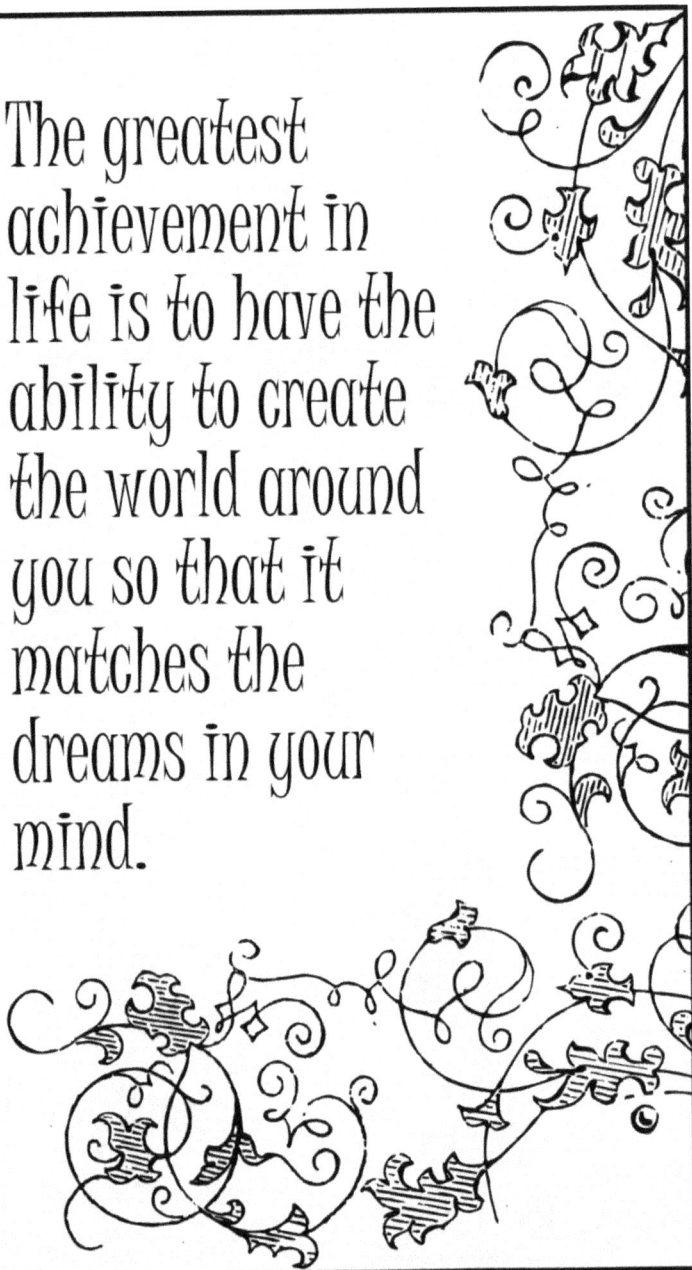

PROVE THEM ALL WRONG.

You are allowed to terminate toxic relationships. You are allowed to walk away from people who hurt you. You are allowed to be angry and selfish and unforgiving. You don't owe anyone an explanation for taking care of yourself.

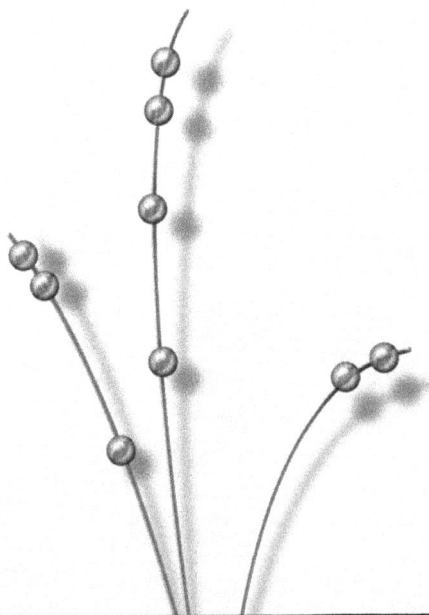

DON'T LOOK BACK.
YOU'RE NOT GOING THAT WAY.

When you feel like quitting,
think about why you started.

Your value doesn't decrease based on someone's inability to see your worth.

What a
wonderful
thought it is
that some of
the best days
of our lives
haven't
happened yet.

PEOPLE WHO SHINE
FROM WITHIN DON'T
NEED THE
SPOTLIGHT.

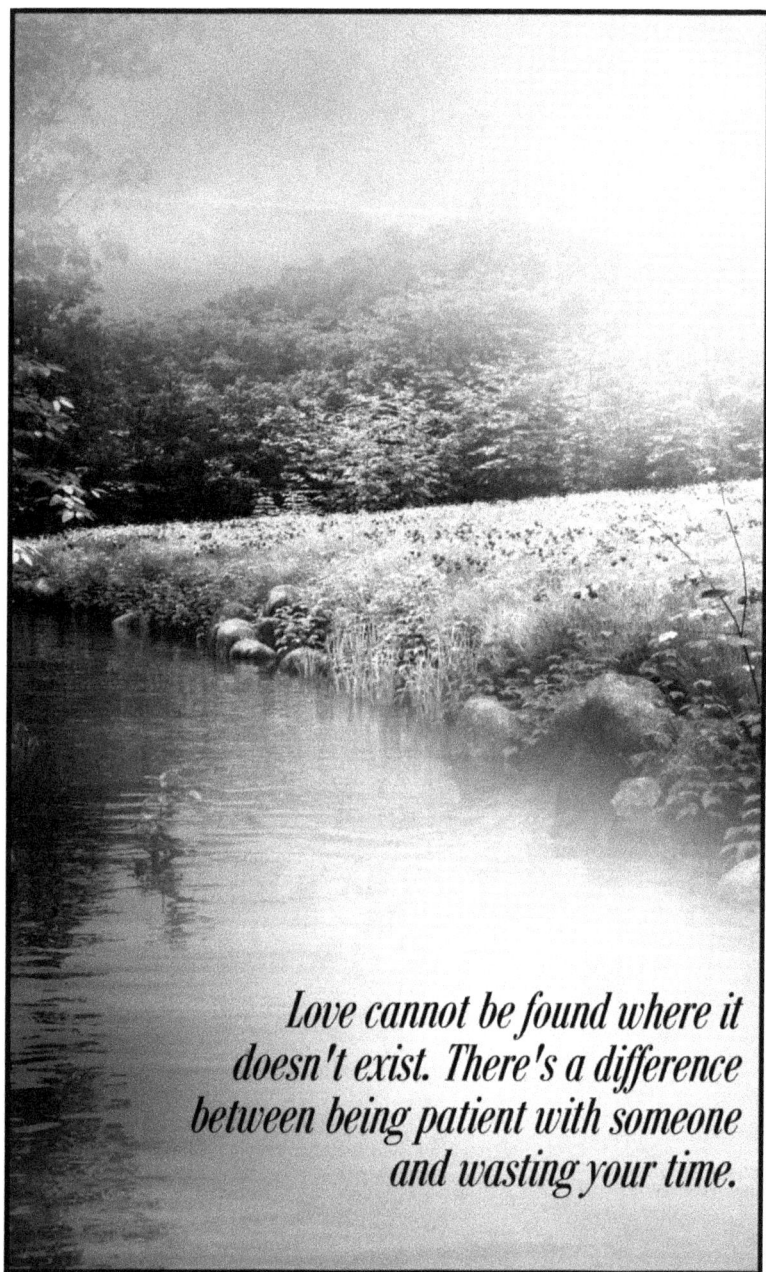

Love cannot be found where it doesn't exist. There's a difference between being patient with someone and wasting your time.

I AM NOT
WHAT I HAVE
DONE, I AM
WHAT I HAVE
OVERCOME.

LIST OF THINGS TO NOT WORRY ABOUT:

1) Stuff I can't control

2) Stuff I can control

What you
allow is
what will
continue.

One reason
people resist
change is because
they focus on
what they have to
give up, rather
than what they
have to gain.

Choose your thoughts wisely for they are the energy that create your life.

BE STRONG.

You never know who you are inspiring.

Life is too long to be miserable.

SEVEN THINGS TO GIVE UP:

1. People pleasing

2. Doubting yourself

3. Negative Thinking

4. Fear of failure

5. Criticizing yourself

6. Saying "Yes" when you want to say "No"

7. Procrastination

THE PEOPLE
YOU
SURROUND
YOURSELF
WITH ARE
CO-CREATING
YOUR LIFE.
CHOOSE YOUR
FELLOW
ARTISTS
CAREFULLY.

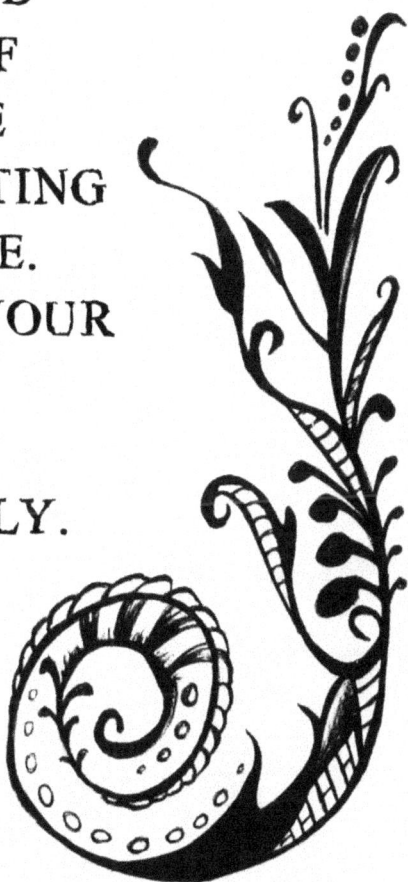

DON'T
BECOME
WHO
HURT
YOU.

Psychologists say, once you learn how to be happy you won't tolerate being around people who make you feel anything less.

YOU'RE NOT GOING TO
PLEASE EVERYONE. STOP
AGONIZING OVER
PERFECTION AND OPEN
YOURSELF TO CREATIVITY.

Attract what you
expect.

Reflect what you
desire.

Become what you
respect.

Mirror what you
admire.

SOMEWHERE ON
THIS PLANET,
THERE IS
SOMEONE
DREAMING THE
LIFE YOU ARE
LIVING RIGHT
NOW.

If it can be solved,
there's no need to
worry.
And if it can't be
solved, worry is of
no use.

SELFISHNESS IS NOT LIVING
YOUR LIFE AS YOU WISH. IT IS
ASKING OTHERS TO LIVE *THEIR*
LIVES AS YOU WISH.

SOMETIMES WE'RE JUST LOYAL
TO THE WRONG PEOPLE.

Stop waiting for approval.
Do what you want and live your life.

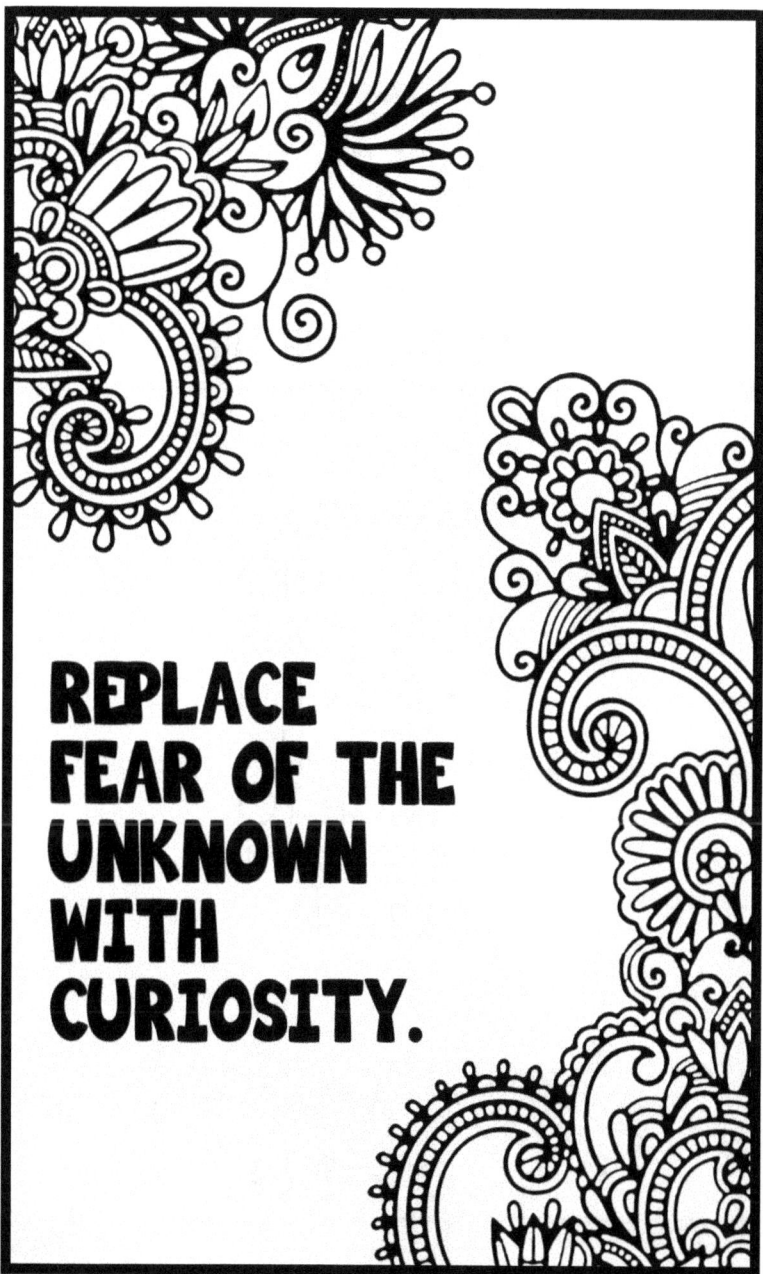

REPLACE FEAR OF THE UNKNOWN WITH CURIOSITY.

IF SOMEONE DID
SOMETHING BAD
ENOUGH TO
MAKE YOU
REMOVE THEM
FROM YOUR
LIFE, DON'T BE
FOOLISH
ENOUGH TO
INVITE THEM
BACK IN.

Stay Strong.

Make them wonder how you're still smiling.

When someone truly cares about you,
they make an effort, not an excuse.

SOMEONE ELSE IS HAPPY WITH LESS THAN WHAT YOU HAVE.

NEVER ALLOW
LONELINESS TO
DRIVE YOU
BACK INTO
THE ARMS OF
SOMEONE YOU
KNOW YOU
DON'T BELONG
WITH.

One of the happiest
moments ever is
when you find the
courage to let go of
what you can't
change.

NEVER GIVE
PERMANENT
FEELINGS TO A
TEMPORARY
PERSON.

STOP TRYING TO
BE "NORMAL"
AND YOU'LL SEE
JUST HOW
AMAZING YOU
ARE.

DRAMA
DOESN'T JUST
WALK INTO
YOUR LIFE OUT
OF NOWHERE.
YOU EITHER
CREATE IT,
INVITE IT, OR
ASSOCIATE
WITH PEOPLE
THAT BRING IT.

Ask yourself if what you are doing today
is getting you closer to where you want
to be tomorrow.

WORRYING WON'T STOP THE
BAD STUFF FROM HAPPENING.
IT JUST STOPS YOU FROM
ENJOYING THE GOOD.

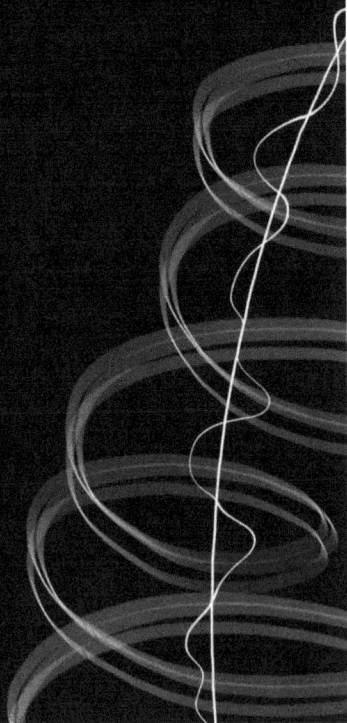

Stop focusing on all the things you don't know how to do and start cultivating the things you do know how to do. You have something beautiful to place in this world. Don't keep it buried inside your soul because you are afraid it's not good enough.

Don't place your mistakes on your
head, their weight may crush you.
Instead, place them under your feet
and use them as a platform to view
your horizons.

TOMORROW -
(noun) a mystical land where 99% of all human productivity, motivation and achievement is stored.

Beware of "Destination Addiction" :

A preoccupation with the idea that happiness is in the next place, the next job or with the next partner. Until you give up the idea that happiness is somewhere else, it will never be where you are.

NOTHING EVER
GOES AWAY
UNTIL IT HAS
TAUGHT US
WHAT WE NEED
TO KNOW.

PEMA CHODRON

TWO THINGS YOU
WILL NEVER HAVE TO
CHASE: TRUE FRIENDS
AND TRUE LOVE.

Mandy Hale

When you say "yes" to others, make sure you are not saying "no" to yourself.

PAULO COELHO

TALKING ABOUT OUR
PROBLEMS IS OUR
GREATEST
ADDICTION.
BREAK THE HABIT.
TALK ABOUT YOUR
JOYS.

RITA SCHIANO

THERE ARE SOME
PEOPLE WHO
ALWAYS SEEM
ANGRY AND
CONTINUOUSLY
LOOK FOR
CONFLICT. WALK
AWAY; THE
BATTLE THEY ARE
FIGHTING ISN'T
WITH YOU, IT IS
WITH
THEMSELVES.

The saddest word in the whole world is the word '*almost*.' He was *almost* in love. She was *almost* good for him. He *almost* stopped her. She *almost* waited. He *almost* lived. They *almost* made it.

NIKITA GILL, *TINY STORIES*

We must be willing to
let go of the life we
planned so as to have
the life that is waiting
for us.

E.M. FORSTER

Believe in your fucking self.
Stay up all fucking night. Work
outside your fucking habits.
Know when to fucking speak up.
Fucking collaborate. Don't
fucking procrastinate. Get over
your fucking self. Keep fucking
learning...Find fucking
inspiration everywhere...Trust
your fucking gut. Ask for
fucking help...Question fucking
everything...Learn to take some
fucking criticism. Make me
fucking care...Do your fucking
research...The problem contains
the fucking solution...Think
about all the fucking possiblities.

BRIAN BUIRGE AND JASON BACHER, CREATORS OF
GOOD FUCKING DESIGN ADVICE

DON'T STUMBLE OVER SOMETHING BEHIND YOU.

Donna L. Watkins

Holding on to anger is like drinking poison and expecting the other person to die.

GAUTAMA BUDDHA

You don't ever have to feel guilty about removing toxic people from your life. It doesn't matter whether someone is a relative, romantic interest, employer, childhood friend, or a new acquaintance -- you don't have to make room for people who cause you pain or make you feel small. It's one thing if a person owns up to their behavior and makes an effort to change. But if a person disregards your feelings, ignores your boundaries, and "continues" to treat you in a harmful way, they need to go.

DANIELL KOEPKE

DON'T LET YOUR HAPPINESS DEPEND ON SOMETHING YOU MAY LOSE.

C.S. LEWIS

FAR TOO MANY PEOPLE
HAVE NO IDEA WHAT THEY
CAN DO BECAUSE ALL
THEY'VE BEEN TOLD IS
WHAT THEY CAN'T DO.

ZIG ZIGLAR

Put all excuses aside and remember this:

YOU ARE CAPABLE.

Zig Ziglar

Protect your spirit from contamination. Limit your time with negative people.

THELMA DAVIS

A GOOD LAUGH AND A
LONG SLEEP ARE THE TWO
BEST CURES FOR ANYTHING.

IRISH PROVERB

Your life is your message to the world. Make sure it's inspiring.

SADY ALI KHAN

THE
BRAVEST
THING I EVER
DID WAS
CONTINUING
MY LIFE
WHEN I
WANTED TO
DIE.

JULIETTE LEWIS

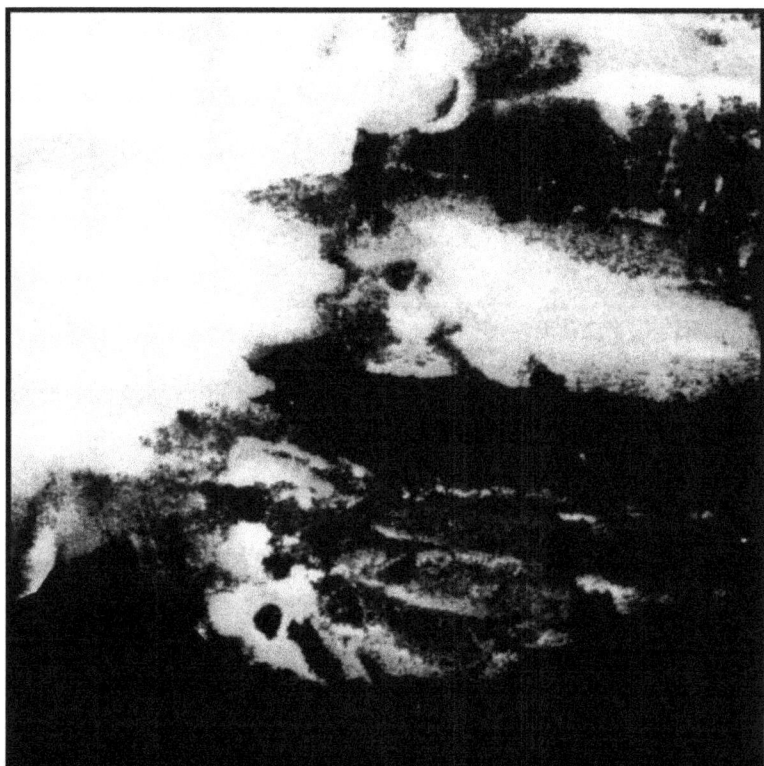

You will not be
punished *for* your
anger. You will be
punished *by* your
anger.

BUDDHA

12 SIGNS IT'S TIME TO MOVE ON FROM A RELATIONSHIP:

1. When you live in past memories more than the present.

2. When the relationship brings you more pain than joy.

3. When he/she expects you to change.

4. When you stay on, expecting he/she will change.

5. When you keep justifying his/her actions to yourself.

6. When he/she is causing you emotional/physical/verbal hurt.

7. When the same situation recurs even though you tried addressing it.

8. When he/she puts little to no effort in the relationship.

9. When your fundamental values and beliefs are different.

10. When the relationship holds you back, hence preventing both of you from growing as individuals.

11. When you stay on expecting things to get better.

12. When neither of you feel the same way about each other.

CELESTINE CHUA, ARTICLE ON LIFEHACK.ORG

As you think, so shall you become.

BRUCE LEE

Have more
than you
show;
speak less
than you
know.

WILLIAM SHAKESPEARE, *KING LEAR*

LEARN TO VALUE
YOURSELF, WHICH
MEANS: FIGHT FOR
YOUR HAPPINESS.

AYN RAND

While we are free to choose our actions, we are not free to choose the consequences of our actions.

STEPHEN R. COVEY

You teach people how to treat you by what you allow, what you stop, and what you reinforce.

TONY GASKINS

Enjoy your youth.
You'll never be
younger than you
are at this very
moment.

CHAD SUGG

Never make someone a priority when all you are to them is an option.

MAYA ANGELOU

Stop the glorification of busy.

GUY KAWASAKI

EVERY ATOM IN YOUR BODY
CAME FROM A STAR THAT
EXPLODED. AND THE ATOMS
IN YOUR LEFT HAND
PROBABLY CAME FROM A
DIFFERENT STAR THAN
YOUR RIGHT HAND. IT
REALLY IS THE MOST
POETIC THING I KNOW
ABOUT PHYSICS. YOU ARE
ALL STARDUST.

LAWRENCE M. KRAUSS, *A UNIVERSE FROM NOTHING:
WHY THERE IS SOMETHING RATHER THAN NOTHING*

When someone loves you, they don't have to say it. You can tell by the way they treat you.

CARSON KOLHOFF

YOU'VE BEEN
CRITICIZING
YOURSELF FOR
YEARS AND IT
HASN'T WORKED.
TRY APPROVING OF
YOURSELF AND SEE
WHAT HAPPENS.

LOUISE HAY

If you're afraid to be hurt again, then you're afraid to be loved again. Don't let hearts that didn't love you keep you from the one that will.

TRENT SHELTON

Waste your money and you're only out of money, but waste your time and you've lost a part of your life.

MICHAEL LEBOEUF

Every
accomplishment
starts with the
decision to try.

GAIL DEVERS

THE ONLY THING
STANDING
BETWEEN YOU AND
YOUR GOAL IS THE
BULLSHIT STORY YOU
KEEP TELLING
YOURSELF AS TO WHY
YOU CAN'T ACHIEVE IT.

JORDAN BELFORT

WHENEVER YOU FEEL SAD
JUST REMEMBER THAT THERE
ARE BILLIONS OF CELLS IN
YOUR BODY AND ALL THEY
CARE ABOUT IS YOU.

RAMANDEEP SINGH

We accept the
love we think we
deserve.

STEPHEN CHBOSKY, *THE PERKS OF BEING
A WALLFLOWER*

People wait all week for Friday,
all year for summer,
all life for happiness.

RITU GHATOUREY

Stop hating
yourself for
everything you
aren't. Start
loving yourself
for everything
that you are.

RITU GHATOUREY

Never give up on
a dream just
because of the
time it will take
to accomplish it.
The time will
pass anyway.

EARL NIGHTINGALE

Never explain.
Your friends don't
need it, and your
enemies won't believe
you anyhow.

ELBERT HUBBARD

You will always be too much of something for someone: too big, too loud, too soft, too edgy. If you round out your edges, you lose your edge. Apologize for mistakes. Apologize for unintentionally hurting someone -- profusely. But don't apologize for being who you are.

DANIELLE LAPORTE

Hate.
It has caused a
lot of problems in
this world, but it
has not solved one
yet.

Maya Angelou

The reason we struggle
with insecurity is
because we compare
our behind-the-scenes
with everyone else's
highlight reel.

STEVE FURTICK

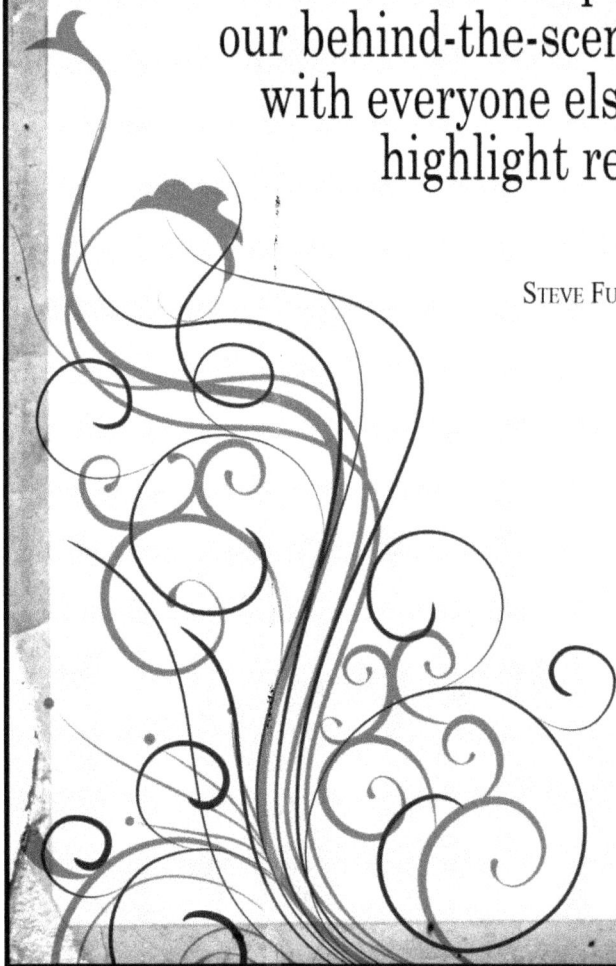

DON'T FALL IN LOVE
WITH SOMEONE WHO
SAYS THE RIGHT THINGS.
FALL IN LOVE WITH
SOMEONE WHO DOES THE
RIGHT THINGS.

ROBERT TEW

A flower does not think of competing with
the flower next to it.
It just blooms.

SENSEI OGUI, ZEN SHIN TALKS

If you want to go fast, go alone.
If you want to go far, go together.

AFRICAN PROVERB

Don't live your life trying to prove to someone what they lost out on. Live for you, freely and purely. Life works itself out...always.

When you complain, you make yourself a victim. Leave the situation, change the situation, or accept it.
All else is madness.

ECKHART TOLE

You cannot control what happens to you, but you can control your attitude toward what happens to you, and in that, you will be mastering change rather than allowing it to master you.

BRIAN TRACY

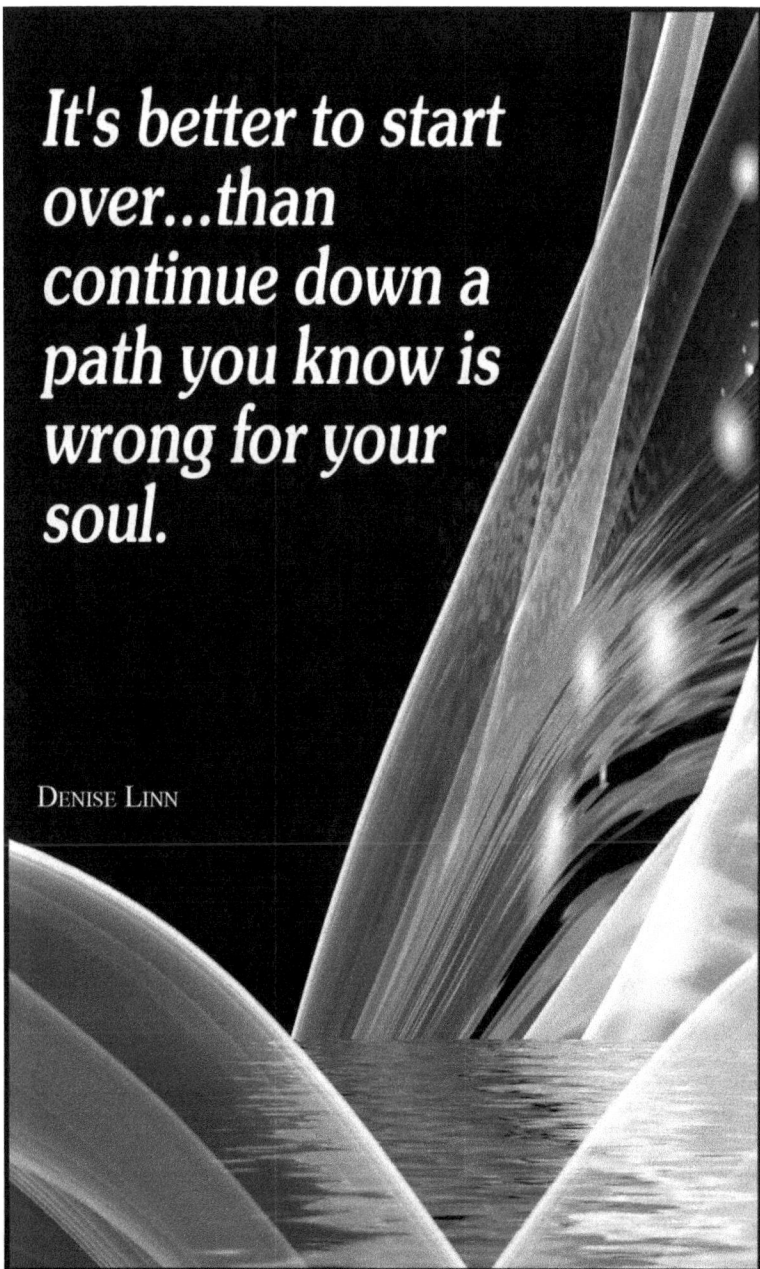

It's better to start over...than continue down a path you know is wrong for your soul.

DENISE LINN

He said, "There are only two days in the year that nothing can be done. One is called yesterday and the other is called tomorrow. So today is the right day to love, believe, do and mostly live."

DALAI LAMA

Crying isn't a sign of weakness. It's a sign of having tried too hard to be strong for too long.

ANURAG PRAKASH RAY

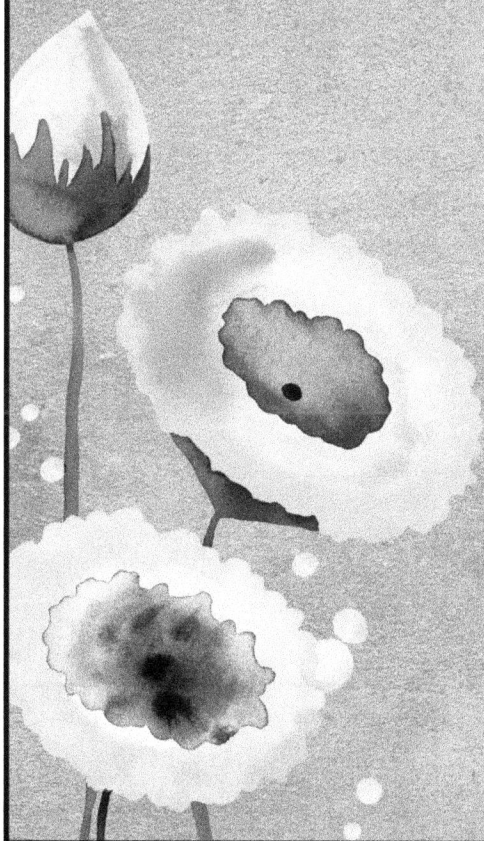

Money is numbers and
numbers never end. If it
takes money to be happy,
your search for happiness
will never end.

BOB MARLEY

The one who follows the crowd will usually go no further than the crowd. The one who walks alone is likely to find himself in places no one has ever been before.

ALAN ASHLEY-PITT

INSTEAD OF BEING
ASHAMED OF WHAT
YOU'VE BEEN
THROUGH, BE PROUD
OF WHAT YOU'VE
OVERCOME.

Dr. Phil

CONFIDENCE IS SILENT.
INSECURITIES ARE LOUD.

You can't expect something different from someone who hasn't done anything to change. Don't stunt your growth waiting on someone who doesn't want to grow with you.

TONY GASKINS, JR.

Self honesty is the greatest honesty because it leads to all significant change.

BILLY COX

DON'T TALK
NEGATIVELY
ABOUT
YOURSELF;
YOU MAY JUST
START TO
BELIEVE IT.

BE CAREFUL WITH YOUR WORDS. ONCE THEY ARE SAID, THEY CAN ONLY BE FORGIVEN, NOT FORGOTTEN.

HUSSEIN NISHAH

HAVE YOU EVER MET
A HATER BETTER
THAN YOU?

ME NEITHER.

THINGS TO KNOW

ABOUT LIFE:

"No" is a complete sentence.
It does not require justification
or explanation.

SELF-WORTH

Some people will like you for no reason; some people will not like you for no reason. Who you choose to spend the most time, thoughts and effort on, depend on exactly how much you like yourself. By just staying near people who treat you poorly, you are telling them it's ok to do so. Only keep people close to you who treat you well.

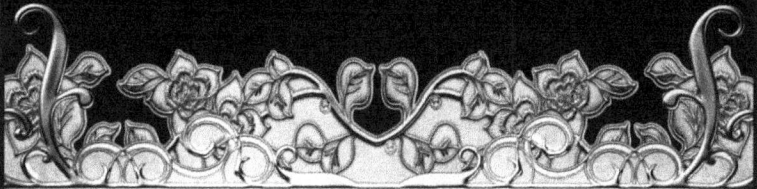

You have the right to forgive yourself any time you want.

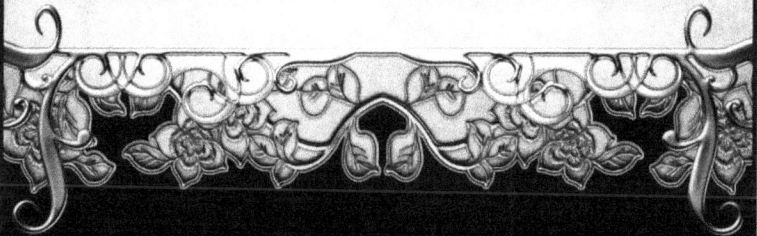

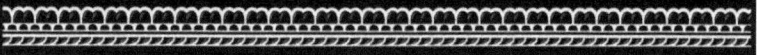

I guess the moment when everything changed was when I realized I deserved so much better.

BEING HAPPY IS
A VERY
PERSONAL THING,
AND IT REALLY
HAS NOTHING TO
DO WITH ANYONE
ELSE.

Just because you haven't got it all figured out doesn't mean you never will. Some day you may even look back and wonder why you were ever worried.

Some people won't love
you no matter what you
do, and some people
won't stop loving you no
matter what you do.

GO WHERE THE LOVE IS!!

DON'T GIVE UP WHAT YOU
WANT MOST FOR WHAT
YOU WANT NOW.

AND IF YOU'RE EVER FEELING LONELY, JUST LOOK AT THE MOON. SOMEONE, SOMEWHERE, IS LOOKING AT IT TOO.

There isn't anything noble about
being superior to another person.
True nobility is in being superior to
the person you once were.

ZIAD K. ABDELNOUR, *ECONOMIC WARFARE: SECRETS OF WEALTH
CREATION IN THE AGE OF WELFARE POLITICS*

Anytime you start a
sentence with

"I AM,"

you are creating what
you are and what you
want to be.

Dr. Wayne Dyer

When nobody else celebrates you, learn to celebrate yourself. When nobody else compliments you, then compliment yourself. It's not up to other people to keep you encouraged. It's up to you. Encouragement should come from inside.

JOEL OSTEEN

REMEMBER:

Today is the tomorrow you
worried about yesterday.

DALE CARNEGIE

No point in stressing over something you can't change. Let it go, move on and grow stronger.

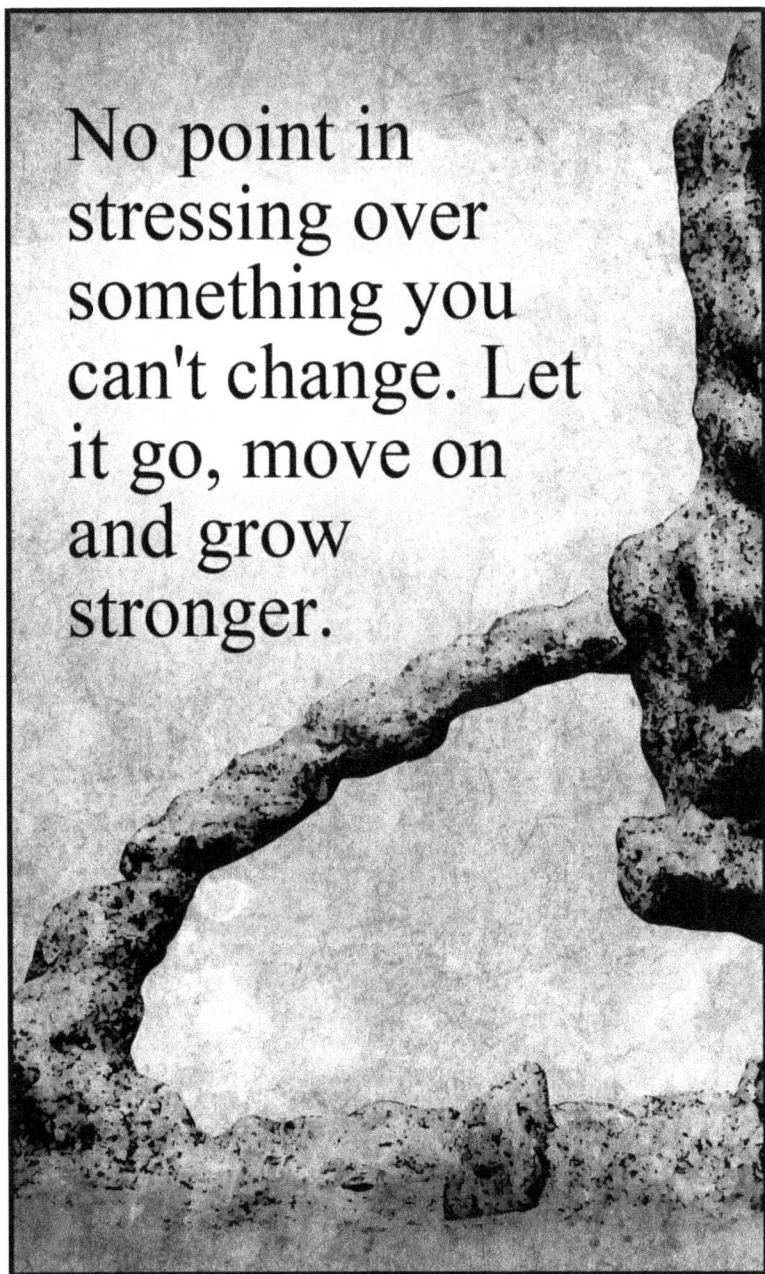

Don't take things personally. What other people say about you is their reality, not yours.

Worrying does not take
away tomorrow's
troubles, it takes away
today's peace.

RANDY ARMSTRONG

The person who says it cannot be done should not interrupt the person doing it.

CHINESE PROVERB

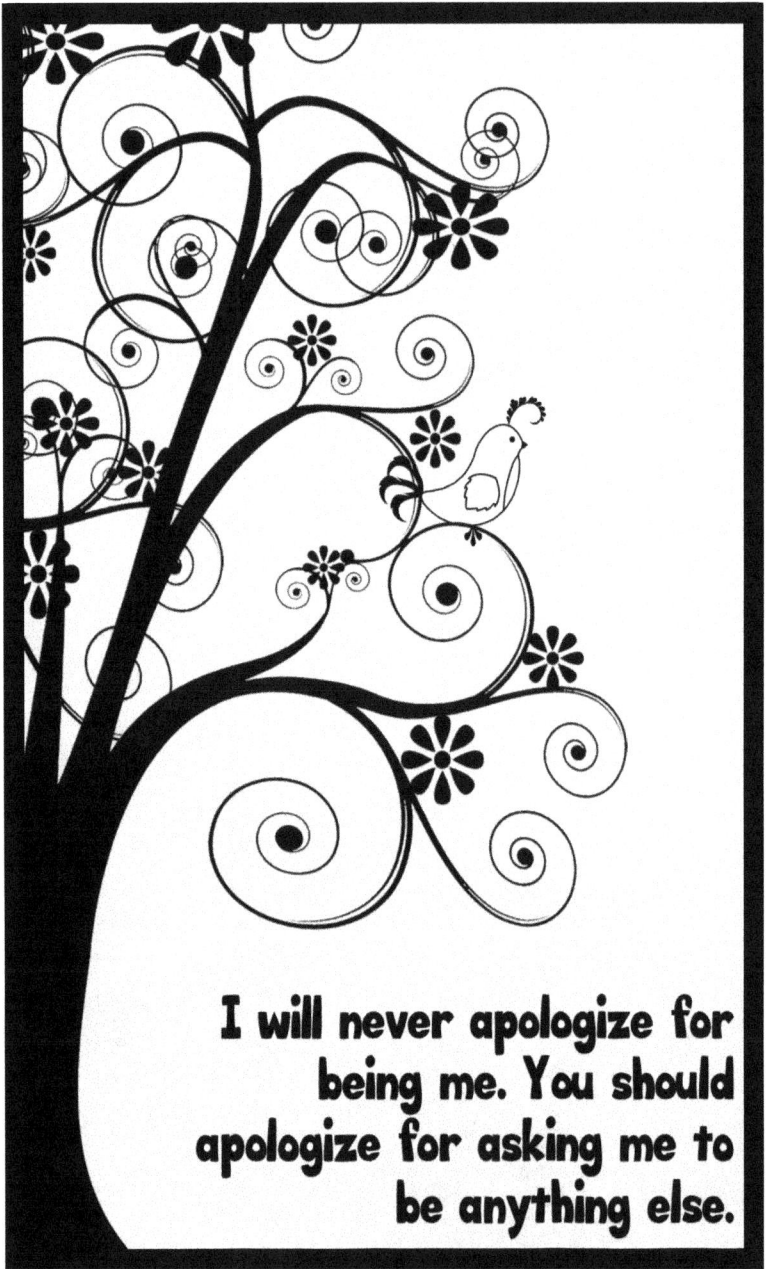

I will never apologize for being me. You should apologize for asking me to be anything else.

Miserable people focus on the things they hate about their life. Happy people focus on the things they love about their life.

SONYA PARKER

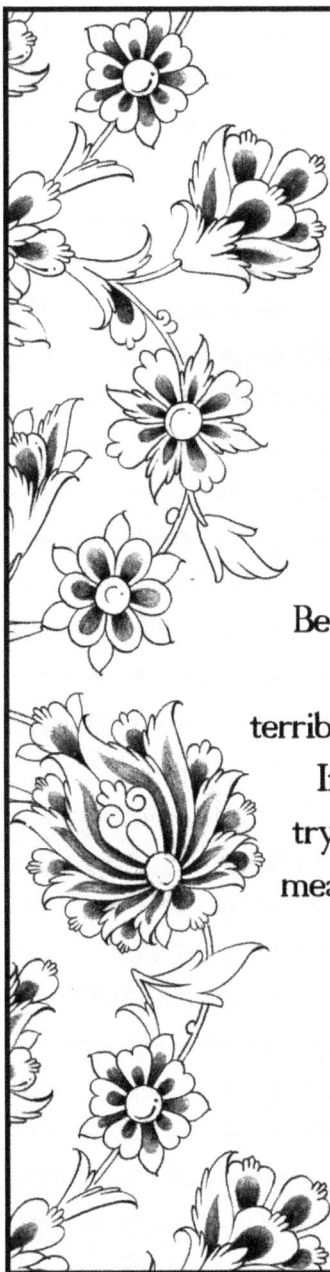

Why?

Because some people are just terrible human beings, and terrible people do terrible things. If you're racking your brain trying to understand it, it just means you're not one of those terrible people.

It's a terrible thing, I think, in life to wait until you're ready. I have this feeling now that actually no one is ever ready to do anything. There is almost no such thing as ready. There is only now. And you may as well do it now. Generally speaking, now is as good a time as any.

HUGH LAURIE

HEY YOU!

YOU'RE PRETTY FUCKING AWESOME.

KEEP THAT SHIT UP.

SERIOUSLY.

Beautiful things happen when you distance yourself from the negative.

DON'T FIGHT FOR
THEIR ATTENTION. IF
THEY REALLY CARE,
YOU SHOULDN'T
HAVE TO.

ROBERT TEW

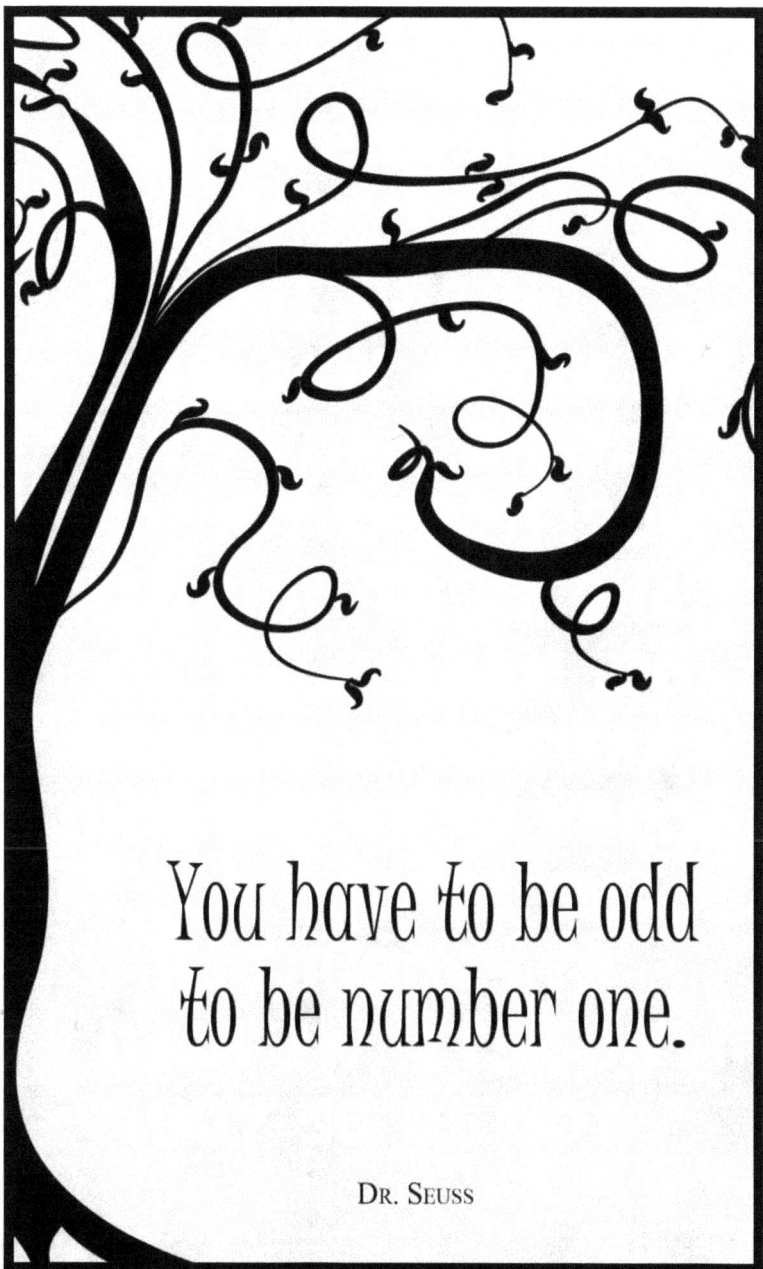

You have to be odd
to be number one.

DR. SEUSS

THERE HAS NEVER
BEEN SOMEONE LIKE
YOU AND THERE
NEVER WILL BE
AGAIN. SHOW THE
WORLD WHO YOU ARE
AND WHAT YOU CAN
DO. MAKE SURE YOU
ARE NOT A CARBON
COPY OF THOSE WHO
CAME BEFORE YOU, A
BY-PRODUCT OF
SOCIETY. WE NEED
YOU TO BE YOU.

Don't compare your path with anybody else's. Your path is unique to you.

RAM DASS

DON'T YOU DARE, FOR ONE MORE SECOND, SURROUND YOURSELF WITH PEOPLE WHO ARE NOT AWARE OF THE GREATNESS THAT YOU ARE.

JO BLACKWELL-PRESTON

Stop saying
"I wish."
Start saying
"I will."

If you're searching for that one person that will change your life, take a look in the mirror.

RITU GHATOUREY

JUST BECAUSE YOU TOOK LONGER THAN OTHERS DOESN'T MEAN YOU FAILED.

It's not other people's job to love you; it's yours. It's important to be nice to others, but it's even more important to be nice to yourself. You really have to love yourself to get anything done in this world. So make sure you don't start seeing yourself through the eyes of those who don't value you. Know your worth, even if they don't.

MARC CHERNOFF, *MARC AND ANGEL HACK LIFE BLOG*

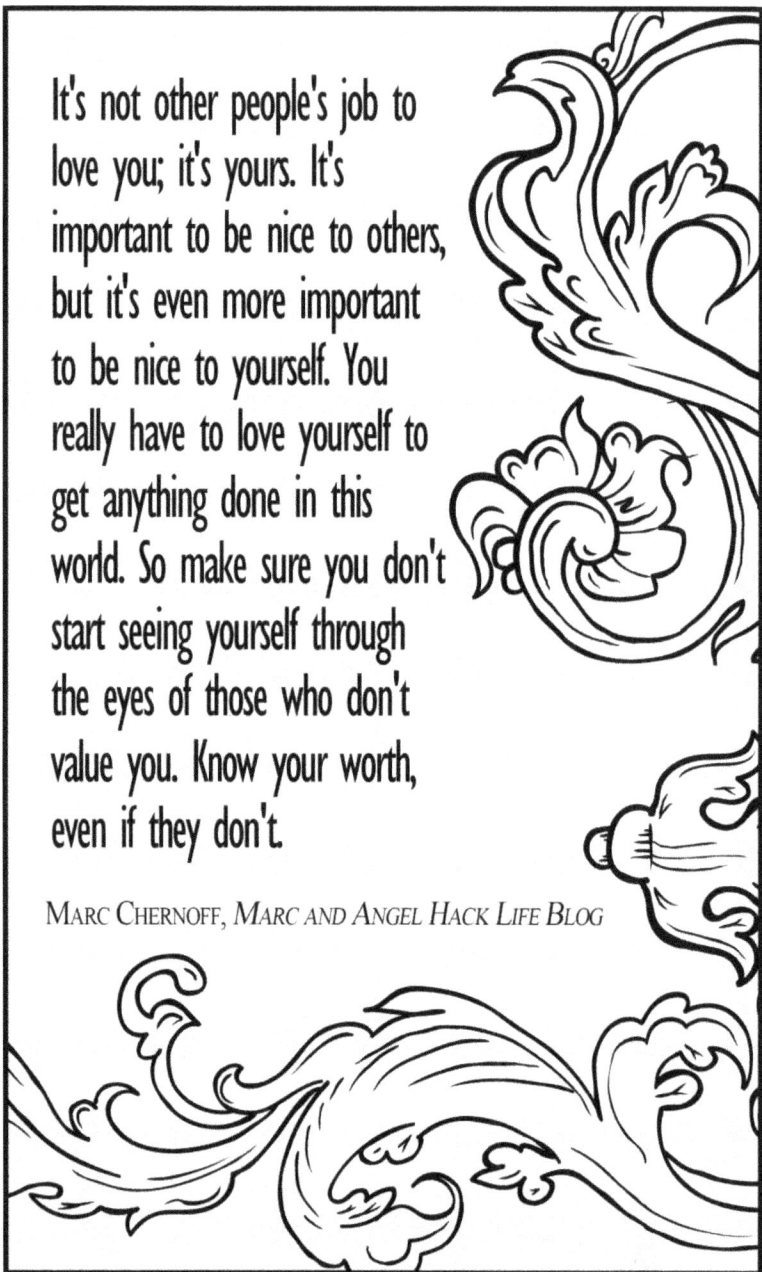

Staying in a
situation where
you're
unappreciated
isn't called
loyalty; it's called
breaking your
own heart.

Stop holding onto people who keep letting go of you. Pay attention to the faithful people. The ones you don't have to impress. The ones who always have your back. The ones that love you with no strings attached.

TRUTH IS, PEOPLE
WHO ARE JEALOUS
OF YOU DON'T EVEN
REALIZE YOU DON'T
HAVE IT ALL
TOGETHER. THEY'RE
ACTUALLY JEALOUS
OF A STRUGGLE
WRAPPED IN
STRENGTH.

In the end, only three things matter:

HOW MUCH YOU
LOVED,
HOW GENTLY YOU
LIVED,
AND HOW
GRACEFULLY YOU
LET GO OF THINGS
NOT MEANT FOR
YOU.

GAUTAMA BUDDHA

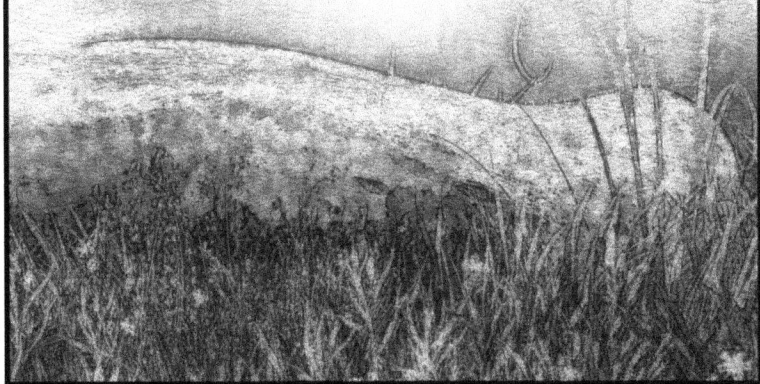

BE CAREFUL HOW
YOU ARE TALKING TO
YOURSELF BECAUSE
YOU ARE LISTENING.

LISA M HAYES

People need to learn that their actions do affect other people. So be careful what you say and do, it's not always just about you.

Be weird. Be random. Be who you are. Because you never know who would love the person you hide.

C.S. LEWIS

My entire life can be described in one sentence:

IT DIDN'T
GO AS
PLANNED,
AND THAT'S
OK.

The worst person to be around is the one who complains about everything and appreciates nothing; the unhappy, negative soul who is quick to find fault with even the best intentions.

REBUILDING YOUR LIFE
FROM WITHIN:

Love yourself unconditionally.

Release your bottled up
emotions.

Make time for long walks alone.

Avoid living beyond your means.

Nurture your inner strength.

Stop apologizing for being you.

Surround yourself with positive
people.

Embrace your situation,
whatever it may be.

Be careful with whatever or whoever you allow yourself to be consumed by.

To be yourself in a world that is constantly trying to make you something else is the greatest accomplishment.

RALPH WALDO EMERSON

Stop looking for
happiness in the same
place you lost it.

If you're giving your all and it's not enough, you're probably giving it to the wrong person.

NOTE TO SELF:

RELAX.

YOU ARE ENOUGH.
YOU HAVE ENOUGH.
YOU DO ENOUGH.

REMEMBER HOW
FAR YOU'VE COME,
NOT JUST HOW
FAR YOU HAVE TO
GO. YOU ARE NOT
WHERE YOU
WANT TO BE, BUT
NEITHER ARE YOU
WHERE YOU USED
TO BE.

RICK WARREN

NEVER QUIT. IF
YOU STUMBLE GET
BACK UP. WHAT
HAPPENED
YESTERDAY NO
LONGER MATTERS.
TODAY'S ANOTHER
DAY. SO GET BACK
ON TRACK AND
MOVE CLOSER TO
YOUR DREAMS
AND GOALS.
YOU CAN DO IT.

SAMIRA FERREIRA

Successful people build each other up. They motivate, inspire and push each other. Unsuccessful people just hate, blame and complain.

There are over 7 billion people on Earth, and you're going to let one person ruin your day?

DON'T.

Don't ever feel bad for
making a decision
about your life that
upsets other people.
You are not responsible
for their happiness.
You're responsible for
your own happiness.
Anyone who wants to
live in misery for their
happiness should not be
in your life to begin
with.

If people are trying to bring
you down, it only means
you are above them.

Just be yourself. Let people see the real, imperfect, flawed, quirky, weird, beautiful, magical person that you are.

MANDY HALE

SOMETIMES WE HAVE TO LET GO OF WHAT'S
KILLING US, EVEN IF IT'S KILLING US TO LET GO.

YOU CAN'T CHANGE HOW
PEOPLE FEEL ABOUT YOU SO
DON'T TRY.

JUST LIVE
YOUR LIFE AND
BE HAPPY.

Life is too short to spend your precious time trying to convince a person who wants to live in gloom and doom otherwise. Give lifting that person your best shot but don't hang around long enough for his or her bad attitude to pull you down. Instead, surround yourself with optimistic people.

ZIG ZIGLAR

Never struggle to
chase love,
affection, or
attention. If it
isn't given freely
by another
person, it isn't
worth having.

NOTE TO SELF:

Every time you were convinced you couldn't go on...

YOU
DID

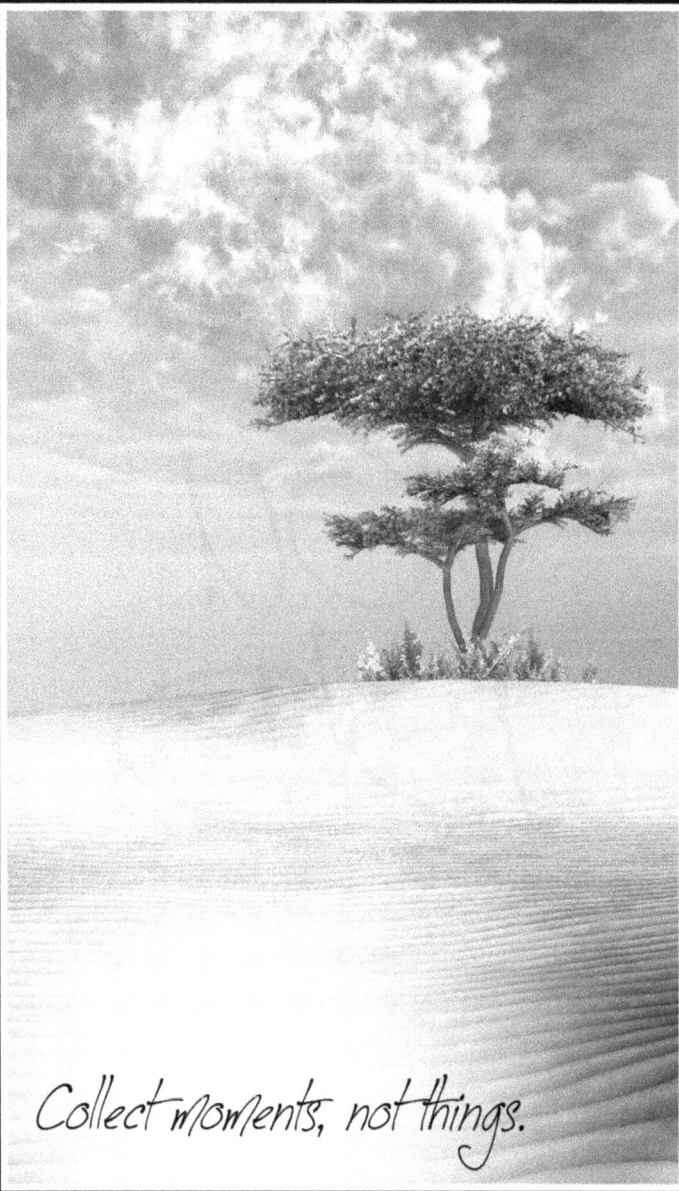

Collect moments, not things.

YOU!

Yes, *YOU*...The one reading this...

You are beautiful, talented, amazing and simply the best at being you.

NEVER FORGET THAT!

One day someone is going to hug you so tight that all of your broken pieces fit back together.

When you talk,
you are only
repeating what you
already know; but
when you listen,
you may learn
something new.

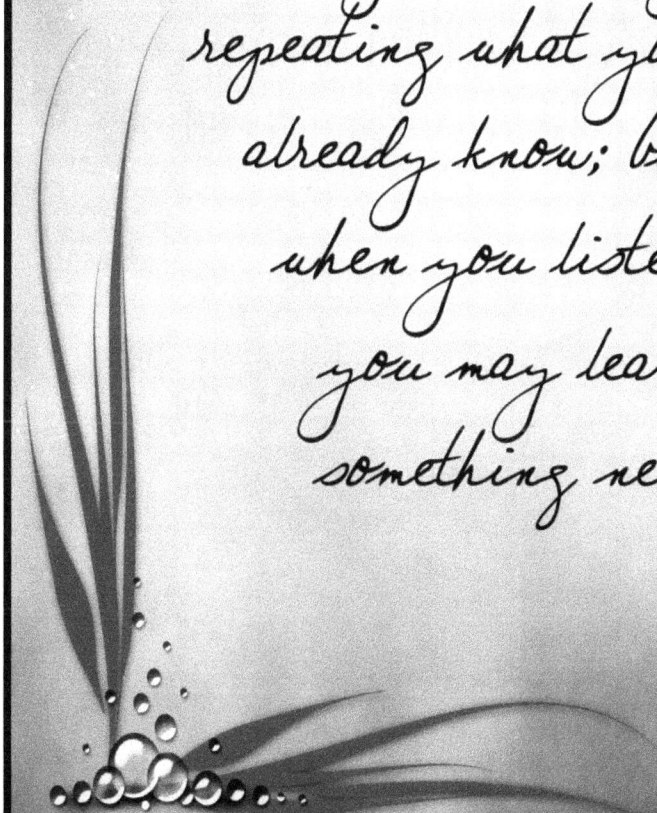

The cost of not following your heart is spending the rest of your life wishing you had.

One day, you'll be just a memory for some people. Do your best to be a good one.

If you are waiting for friends, your husband or wife, employer, employees or co-workers to give you what you want, you are turning your power over to others...you are setting yourself up for possible disappointment.

SANAYA ROMAN AND DUANE PACKER,
CREATING MONEY: KEYES TO ABUNDANCE

www.ingramcontent.com/pod-product-compliance
Lightning Source LLC
Chambersburg PA
CBHW071051040426
42443CB00013B/3308